CW00447198

REFLECTIONS OF A RIFLEMAN

One of the author's own coloured drawings pasted into the manuscript. His monogram WEJ is after the words Advance Post. It illustrates Reflection 2, The Ridge at Vimy. The soldier on the left is using a Lewis machine gun

REFLECTIONS OF A RIFLEMAN

An East Londoner's experiences of the First World War

Walter Edward James

Valence House Publications
2021

Published in 2021 by Valence House Publications
Valence House, Becontree Avenue
Dagenham, Essex RM8 3HT

www.valencehousecollections.co.uk

ISBN 978-1-911391-09-8

Copyright statement:
The original manuscript and its contents are ©the family of Walter
Edward James
The introduction and all editorial material is ©Valence House
Publications

All rights reserved. No part of this book may be reproduced or
transmitted in any form or by any means, electronic or
mechanical, including photocopying, recording or by any
information storage or retrieval system, without the written
permission of the copyright holders

VALENCE HOUSE
a place of discovery

Valence House is the home of the London Borough of Barking
and Dagenham's Museum, Archives and Local Studies
Centre. It is a focus for local community heritage projects in
which professional staff encourage enthusiastic volunteers to
use their natural talents and learned skills for mutual benefit

CONTENTS

FOREWORD

My name is Valerie Fincham and I am the granddaughter of Walter Edward James. I became the curator of his manuscript memoir after the recent death of my mother, his daughter Violet. It is handwritten into an exercise book. It also contains his own coloured drawings and a few photographs, cuttings and other documents.

Walter was born 9th July 1889 in Felstead Street, Hackney Wick, to Henry James, a carpenter and decorator from Birmingham, and his wife Harriet. Soon afterwards the family moved the short distance to Shoreditch. Walter followed his father into the painting and decorating trade. On Christmas Day 1913 he married Emily Lilian Scrimshaw and the following year their daughter Emily was born.

In September 1916, while Walter was serving in the trenches at the Somme, his wife gave birth to a premature son, Walter Frederick, who only lived two weeks. Tragically, their daughter Emily died of meningitis in November 1918, a few days after the Armistice.

After the war the couple settled back into everyday life, living first at Pearson Street before moving to Weymouth Terrace in the early 1930s. They had two further children, Walter Edward (known as Ted) in 1919 and Violet in 1927. Walter died in July 1942 aged 53.

Reflections of a Rifleman is an astonishingly vivid first-hand account of major conflicts on the Western Front and in Palestine during the Great War of 1914-18. As well as the sights and sounds of battle, Walter gives us small details of the day-to-day life and comradeship of soldiers enduring horrors we can hardly imagine.

Walter had a passion for education and encouraged his daughter Violet to win a LCC scholarship to the prestigious Christ's Hospital boarding school in Hertford. Violet (later Mrs Gasson) went on to train as a teacher, working at Hogarth Primary School in Brentwood and St Edward's Church of England Primary School in Romford.

This is the first time my grandfather's memoir has been published to a wider audience. I think it's important to pass on to the next generation what 'ordinary' people such as him, a self-educated East End house painter, went through and what they thought of war.

My own next generation are two daughters, two grandsons, one new granddaughter, a niece and a nephew. Reading this book will bring them closer to their ancestor of a century ago and I know they will be proud of him.

Valerie Fincham
October 2021

Walter's great-great-grandsons at Vimy, where he fought in 1916

INTRODUCTION

Walter Edward James's service record has not survived, but other sources together with this memoir enable us to reconstruct the essentials. The Silver War Badge document shows that he enlisted on 13th July 1915 and was given the service number 322019. The following four months were spent training in this country.

According to the Service Medal and Award Rolls, his periods of active service abroad ("in a theatre of war") were as follows:

With the 6th Battalion London Regiment (The City of London Rifles), known as the Cast Iron Sixth due to historic links with the printing trade, from 13th November 1915 to 17th January 1916 and from 1st April 1916 to 9th June 1917.

This is followed by active service with the 2nd Battalion 16th London Regiment (Queen's Westminster Rifles) from 28th November 1917 to 17th June 1918 and from 21st June 1918 to 26th September 1918.

Reading the memoir, it becomes clear that the gaps in these dates are explained by his spells of sick leave in this country. The Silver War Badge document states that he was discharged on 1st March 1919.

These Reflections are extraordinarily vivid and direct. Not a word is wasted. It's as if Walter (known as Jimmy to his mates) sits opposite us inside Dirty Dick's in Shoreditch (mentioned in Reflection 3), asking "Want to know what life was like for the ordinary Tommy at Loos, Vimy, the Somme, Ypres, Passchendaele and Palestine?

Fetch me a pint of bitter and I'll tell you". His account is full of Cockney humour, a bit of ducking and diving, stoicism in the face of great danger of death, and a sympathetic attitude towards the German and Turkish soldiers on the other side who, like him, were trapped in a tragic mess not of their own making. The only group he refers to as "our mortal enemies" are the Redcaps, the British military police!

It's important to remember that this work is **not** a diary or a complete narrative of Walter's wartime experiences. The title Reflections sums up his intention – to describe the particular episodes that remained most vivid in his mind long after the event. He set the Reflections down on paper many years afterwards, possibly as late as the early 1930s. Unfortunately none of his original wartime letters, notes or diaries appear to have survived.

Because of the long interval, Walter's memory may have slightly reshaped some events. We've noticed occasional discrepancies when checking dates and names in his Reflections against official sources such as the Commonwealth War Graves Commission website. We discuss this further in the Appendix (page 83).

The memoir begins in December 1915, in the aftermath of the Battle of Loos. The mention of "the tragic affair of September 25th" refers to the first day of that battle. It was the first mass attack of the war and Walter's battalion, the Cast Iron Sixth, had suffered huge losses.

Linda Rhodes
October 2021

ACKNOWLEDGEMENTS

The text was transcribed from the original manuscript by Valerie Fincham, Deirdre Marculescu and Linda Rhodes

Additional research by David Porter

Files prepared for publication by Derek Alexander

Family history information supplied by Valerie Fincham and Amy McCarthy

We extend our thanks to staff of the following:

London Borough of Hackney Archives

Valence House Archives & Local Studies Centre (LBBD)

London Borough of Havering Libraries (Local Studies)

Supplementary sources

The Cast Iron Sixth war diaries held at the National Archives form a vital contemporary record of the activities of the battalion. They can be read on the Ancestry website (search under Piece Description 2729/1-7)

E.G. GODFREY: The Cast Iron Sixth: a history of the Sixth Battalion, London Regiment (The City of London Rifles). Published 1938. A facsimile reprint has been issued by the Naval & Military Press (ISBN 978-1-843421702)

Internet sites consulted include

Commonwealth War Graves Commission www.cwgc.org
Ancestry www.ancestry.co.uk
Find My Past www.findmypast.co.uk
The Genealogist www.thegenealogist.co.uk

ABBREVIATIONS

C.B.	Confined to Barracks
C.S.M.	Company Sergeant Major
M.O.	Medical Officer
N.C.O.	Non-Commissioned Officer
P.H. gas helmets	Phenate Hexamine gas masks
R.A.M.C.	Royal Army Medical Corps
R.F.C.	Royal Flying Corps
R.S.M.	Regimental Sergeant Major
R.T.O.	Railway Transport Officer
S.M.	Sergeant Major
YMCA	Young Men's Christian Association

MILITARY SLANG:

NAPOO (from the French "il n'y a plus", or "none left") meant both "finished" (e.g. with regard to rations), and "dead" (when talking about fellow soldiers).

A NOTE ON THE TEXT

The words contained in these pages are exactly as Walter James wrote them a century ago. However, we have occasionally amended punctuation, capitalisation and spelling for the sake of clarity for the modern reader.

Walter James with his father Henry, who was serving in the Royal Defence Corps

Walter's parents, Henry and Harriet James

Reflection No 1
A POSH TIME AT LOOS

December 20th 1915

We are going up into the line again. Our platoon sergeant, Tattersall, known to the lads of No 1 Platoon as "Taters", tells me we are going up to trenches near the Hohenzhollern Redoubt in the Hulluch sector, not far from Loos, the scene of the tragic affair of September 25th.

We fall in outside the estanque in the village of Sailly-Labourse, where we have been resting for four days. The rumour is going round that we are going in for four days. We shall be back again in billets for Christmas. We live in hopes, but we know these rumours, we almost live on them. Rumours of this, rumours of that...Jerry is asking for peace terms, we are going back to Blighty to be re-formed, we are going to Egypt, we are going out to the Italian Front. Rumours, rumours and then more rumours.

It is now three o'clock, a cold dry morning. We parade in full pack wearing gum thigh boots, our walking boots being fastened by the laces to our valises. Each man looks like a loaded camel. Loaves of French bread, pieces of bully beef boxes, parcels that have recently arrived from Blighty hang on the equipment of most of us.

Each man carries two hundred rounds of ammunition, a valise packed with greatcoat, spare shirts and socks, towel, pants etc., haversack containing holdall with knife, fork, spoon, razor and various other articles, and also emergency rations generally called Iron Rations. A full water bottle, rifle and bayonet, entrenching tool and two P.H. gas helmets and a waterproof ground sheet. The weight of the entire outfit cannot be far short of a hundred pounds.

The platoon officer, Second Lieutenant Graves, arrives. Taters gives a brisk salute. "All present and correct, Sir".

"Very good, Sergeant. Platoon, form fours. Right, quick march".

We move off like a platoon of ghosts in the darkness of the winter morning, our gumboots making no sound on the rough cobbled stones of the village street. Only the rattle of entrenching tools against rifle butts or the voice of a man speaking to his comrade break the silence. On we go through the deserted village along the open country road, through the shell-bashed village of Noyelles, on through the tragic battered village of Vermelles.

Now we move in single file. An eighteen-pounder battery suddenly crashes out a salvo from behind the ruins of a shattered farmhouse. The order comes down "No noise, no smoking". A man curses as he crashes into a shell hole.

We enter the communication trench. A board sticks out just below the parapet with the name Chapel Alley on it. On we go, past dugouts from which the lights of candles pierce the gloom, and from which comes a warm earthy smell. Our packs are beginning to feel like a ton weight. Past another dugout. A man is lounging in the entrance. "What mob are you, mate?" I answer quietly "The Londons".

The order comes down "Keep close in to the right, stretcher party coming along". We hug the wall of the trench as the stretcher bearers pass with their burden. I glance at the wounded man as the bearers push by. His face is swathed in bandages. He looks bad, but anyway it's a cert Blighty. Still on we go.

It is now getting near daybreak. We have been tramping for over three hours already. We reach the line at last. The men we have relieved file out. We dump our packs, sentries are told off and the remainder are free to snatch an hours rest in a dugout or on the fire-step. We are in the front line near the famous Hohenzhollern Redoubt.

It is Christmas Eve. It has been raining continuously for the last two days and the trenches are knee deep in water and mud that sticks to you like your defaulter's sheet in the record office. I have just been relieved from sentry duty and have crawled into a hole in the parapet of the trench that passes for a dugout. It has a layer of mud several inches deep on the floor of it. You cannot stand up in it and it is about four feet square. From behind the rotting timbers of its roof a couple of well-fed looking rats are taking a great interest in my movements. The thought comes into my mind that there are worse things than being a rat.

I hang my rifle on a piece of jutting timber and begin searching in my haversack for a small tin of cocoa that I have received from home. A mess tin of cocoa will warm me up for I am soaked to the skin and am a mass of mud. The lice inside my shirt and pants seem to be working overtime too, but I have often noticed the more cold and wretched you feel, the more they bite. Surely the motto of these pests must be "I will never leave thee or forsake thee".

I find a couple of candles which I light and stick up on the lid of my mess tin, this being the only suitable place in the dugout dry enough for this purpose. And then half-filling the main part of my mess tin with water from my water bottle, I squat down in the mud and hold it over the two small flames. It will be a long job I know, but perhaps the water will be hot enough before I have to go on sentry again.

I light an issue fag and wonder what the people at home are thinking about on this eve of Christmas. We are supposed to be relieved in the morning, but there seems to be a doubt about it. The rats in the roof start squealing and scampering about and a lump of mud drops with a plop into my mess tin. Never mind, it will all mix up when it boils.

My mate "Tug" Wilson crawls through the entrance, bringing yet more mud with him. He has got a grievance. Taters has warned him for fatigue in a quarter of an hour's time to help repair a part of the C.S.M. dugout which has collapsed. He is calling the S.M. and Taters more fancy names than I have got gaspers in my cigarette case.

He is just on the point of starting a fresh list when there is a terrific crash and half the roof of the dugout descends on us. Taters is shouting outside "Stand to, everybody!" We grasp our rifles and scramble into the trench which Jerry is plastering with shrapnel, and mounting our fire-step await orders, which soon arrive for Lieutenant Graves comes staggering through the mud shouting "Rapid Fire!"

We carry on loading and firing until our rifles are almost too hot to handle. After a time we get the order to cease fire and stand down from the fire steps but to remain standing to in the trench. Taters gives us the information that Jerry has blown up a mine on our immediate flank and that an attack is expected. We are given more ammunition. It is still raining. We get permission to clean our rifles.

It is the evening of Christmas Day. It is still raining and we are still standing to. We have had no rations since we stood to. I found a few pieces of biscuit in my haversack and have had a nibble at them occasionally. Jerry is very quiet. I believe I have taken root in the mud. I do not seem to have any feet. They seem as if they are dead and buried. Why the hell do they keep us standing to like this?

Tug Wilson, next to me in the slime, is moaning. "Christ, wot a bleedin' Christmas. Ain't we ever goin' ter 'av any perishin' grub agin? Oh Blimey, why did I ever join up ter be messed abaht like this 'ere? I bet ole Jerry's nice and snug in 'is dugout, knockin' back 'is Christmas rootie and ere's us silly basterds playin' stick in ther mud. Wot wouldn't I give nar for a mug of 'ot corfee, and a plate of sossidge an' mash".

I tell him to put a sock in it and try to ease one of my legs from the vice-like grip of the mud. I am beginning to feel rather queer and light-headed.

I seem to have dozed off or swooned when I hear a voice, as from a distance. "Stand down!" And then Tug's voice "Cum on Jimmy. D'yer stan' dahn. Wassa matter? Carn't yer move?"

"Tug" Wilson, next to me in the slime, is moaning "Christ! wot a bleedin' Christmas ... aint we ever goin' ter 'av any perishin' grub. agin .... Oh Blimey why did I ever join up ter be messed abaht like this 'ere ... I bet ole Jerrys nice and snug in 'is dug-out knockin' back 'is Christmus rootie and 'eres us silly barsterds playin' stuck in ther mud -- wot would'nt I giv' nar for a mug of 'ot corfee and a plate of Sossidge an' mash" I tell him to "put a sock in it"

I am in the field ambulance at Sailly-Labourse. I have been taken here with pineapple feet caused through standing in mud and waters. Tug Wilson and another mate had to pull me out of the sticky mess on Christmas night. I had no use in my feet so I was taken out on a stretcher. Somehow or other I sustained a badly cut lip (probably while being tugged out of the mud).

Anyhow, when the doctor came to see me this morning he looked at my cut lip and then at my boxing glove feet and said with a twinkle in his eye "Ah, what have we here? A case of foot and mouth disease eh! Mark him down for the base".

"*Reflections of*
a. Rifleman"

№ 2

"*On The Ridge of Vimy*"

THE HILL OF NOTRE DAME DE LORETTE
WITH THE BATTERED CHURCH OF
ABLAIN S⁺ NAZARE·· NEAR THE VIMY RIDGE

Reflection No 2

ON THE RIDGE OF VIMY

On the 20th May 1916 we left our billets to proceed up the line to take over trenches on the Vimy Ridge. It was a glorious summer day and we all felt in good spirits as we made our way through Villers-au-Bois and through the line of trenches known as Cabaret Rouge.

I had not long returned from Blighty where I had been for a short time in hospital and on sick leave as a result of my trench feet sustained at Loos on Christmas.

There are several strange faces in the platoon and we have got a new platoon commander, Lieutenant Wiley, who is a good sort. My mate Tug Wilson is also still with us.

The usual rumours are going round, and it is generally believed that we are going to a hot shop, but that doesn't worry us over much. Plenty of time to worry about that when we get there, which I hope won't be too long, as it is rather hot and the pack, as usual, seems to weigh a ton.

Eventually we arrive at the reserve trenches which two companies of the battalion take over. Our company is to take over the support line and very soon I, with the rest of my section, are in possession of a kind of lean-to dugout, which somewhat resembles a large hen house with a couple of layers of sandbags on the top.

Hardly have we got our packs off when Taters, our platoon sergeant, is round warning some of us for various duties. I am lucky, for my name is not called, but as usual,

Tug Wilson falls in for it and goes out of the dugout with his usual angel-like expressions.

Another member of our section, Powell, is busy diving in his valise. Soon he produces a brown paper parcel which he unties and then produces a various assortment of articles which he places on his ground sheet. Idly I glance at the assortment, which consists of packets of chocolate, toffee, cigarettes, vaseline, Harrison's Pomade (faithfully believed in by loving relatives in Blighty as the unfailing remedy for killing that bosom friend of the soldier on active service – lice – but just as firmly recognized by the soldier himself as a handy substitute for rifle oil or petroleum jelly, when cleaning his rifle).

Soon Powell (or Pole Cat as he is called by most of us, for he is not the ideal clean soldier) is stuck into a great slab of chocolate. The Pole Cat is a greedy cuss. He has never been known to offer any one of us anything from the contents of a parcel. He would be quite happy lying on a dung-heap with plenty of toffee, chocolate and cake to eat. Nothing ever seems to worry him. He is a tall, weedy sort of a chap with a dirty-looking complexion, and as much like a soldier as a rat is like a racehorse.

There he sprawls beside his ground sheet with one hand thrust inside his tunic, scratching his chest. It is generally understood that the Pole Cat is always in possession of the finest collection of lice in the whole battalion. Even when there is a chance of a bath he does his utmost to dodge it. He never seems to try to make a friend of any of us and none of the section certainly make any effort to enrol him as a mate.

Sitting on his pack a little distance from him is Jimmy Hurst, one of the oldest members of the platoon. He came out with the battalion in March 1915 and was with them at Festubert and Loos. He is by way of being something of a boxer, and I have had many a set-to with the gloves with him when we have been out of the line.

He coolly bends forward and helps himself to a cigarette from a box lying on the Pole Cat's ground sheet. "What about 'anding those fags round, yer greedy swine? Yer know we're nearly all napoo of issues. 'Ow the bleedin' 'ell yer can sprawl there and never 'orfer any of us a fag or a bit of choclit fair beats me". His eyes rove round the dugout invitingly to all of us. "Nar if there's any of you blokes short of a fag, I invites you, on behalf of my friend 'ere, the Right 'Onerable Pole Cat, 'ter cum forward and help yourselves. But wait er minit, I'll save yer the trouble. Keep yer seats gents, and I'll cum rahnd an 'and em out to yer".

At this threatened attack on his property the Pole Cat scrambles to his feet, but is neatly tripped up by Jimmy and crashes down on top of his ground sheet. By the time he regains his feet we have all lit up our "presentation" fag and the empty box is handed back to him.

At this moment our section leader Lance Corporal Jackson enters and tells us to fall in outside. The Pole Cat hastily rolls up the remainder of the contents of his parcel, snatches up his rifle and follows us out into the trench.

It is the afternoon of the next day, May 21st. We are all in our hen-coop dugout – that is, all with the exception of those who are on some duty or other in the trench.

Tug Wilson and Jimmy Hurst have started a game of House. This game consists of two men, one of whom holds a bag out of which the other pulls discs with numbers on. As he pulls each number out he shouts what it is. The remainder of the players all have cards which they have bought off the two who are running the bank, for twopence. These cards bear three lines of numbers, about fifteen, in rows of five.

As the numbers are called out any player who has that number on his card covers the number with a small stone or piece of paper, or anything like that which happens to be handy. The first player who gets one complete row of five numbers covered up in this way shouts out "House!"

The numbers are checked by the two workers and if found correct they pay the house money to the winner. The amount of house money varies of course, according to the amount of players. Thus if there were, say, twelve players with cards at twopence each, the winner would get about fifteen pence, the remainder being kept by the two workers.

Behold us then on this May afternoon, squatting on the floor of our palatial dugout with our cards in front of us listening to the chant of the worker as he calls out the numbers from his canvas bag. Number ten. Clickety-click, sixty-six. Number twelve. Kelly's Eye, number one. Legs eleven. Blind half-hundred, fifty. Top of the House, one hundred. Dirty spree, thirty-three. Catch 'em alive, number five, and so forth.

The first game is won, of all persons, by the Pole Cat, and the second game immediately begins. We have been playing for some considerable time when we become aware of the fact that Jerry is sending over an unusual amount of greetings. We, however, think it is the usual afternoon strafe and that it won't last long.

On with the game. Number eight. Rory O'More, number four. Me and you, number two. Number fifteen. Ain't it fine, number nine. Number seven. Number twenty-six. "Blimey, old Fritz ain't half sending over some good wishes".

Clickety-click. Top o' the House. "Christ, it's getting a bit peasy ain't it?"

Number twen'y-five. Fourteen. Twenny-eight. Firty-six. The bombardment is increasing. The game of House comes to a stop.

Jimmy Hurst looks out of the dugout entrance. "There's somethin' coming 'orf, bet yore bleedin' life". His words are drowned by a tremendous crash as a big shell drops on the company cookhouse dugout close by us, completely demolishing it. Immediately there arises a cry of "Stretcher bearers!"

A couple of bearers with a stretcher arrive and we help them to dig out the occupants of the shattered cookhouse. Dick Lloyd and his assistant cook "Sailor" Richards will never again cook a bully beef stew. Against the shattered wall of the trench a man is lying face to the ground. It is Lance Corporal Jackson.

The shelling is increasing in volume. Jerry is putting down a complete curtain of fire on our sector, cutting us off from all hopes of support from right or left. We crouch down in the bottom of the trench, wishing we were worms that we might burrow deep down into the earth. It is very evident this is the prelude to an attack.

The word is passing down, "Gas helmets on!" Jerry is sending over tear-shells. I get a dose of it before I can get my mask on. My eyes feel as if they have been rubbed with onions. No orders come along. We simply crouch where we are, waiting for something to happen.

After a time the word is passed down for company bombers. I am a company bomber, so with the other bombers of the company we stagger over the debris into the communication trench. We are under the command of our platoon sergeant, Taters. Our job is to make a sandbag block across the communication trench and hold it against Jerry, who has taken our front line and is expected to bomb his way down to take the support trench.

A man of B Company is lying flat on his back in the trench. He has no tunic or cap on. The expression on his face is ghastly. He has evidently been killed by a bayonet thrust through the stomach. How he comes to be without his tunic I cannot understand.

I do not know the man's name, but I know him by sight as a man who frequently sang at battalion concerts. One of his songs comes into my mind as I stare at him, watching the flies buzzing in and out of his open mouth. A sentimental song. Some of the words went:

> Some day when dreams come true
> Some time in the future years
> I'll come back to you dear heart,
> Love shining through the tears.

It is two o'clock next morning. The bombardment has slackened down considerably. Taters has gone back to the main body of the platoon, who are digging a new trench just in front of the battered support line. I, with two other bombers, one of whom is the Pole Cat and the other Tug Wilson, are left to hold the "block", or sandbag barricade. We are taking it in turns to do half hours watching while the other two rest. It is my half hour, and I stand looking over the barricade with a Mills grenade ready to hand.

Tug is stretched on his back in the trench with his eyes closed, but I don't know whether he is asleep or not. The Pole Cat is crouched up against the wall of the trench munching at a slab of chocolate. If Jerry had suddenly appeared and snaffled the three of us, I don't think it would have made any impression on him.

We have had nothing to eat for some considerable time. I would have been glad of a piece of that chocolate, but I know the Pole Cat would never think of parting with any. I am just thinking of telling him to come over and take my place at the block, when a hand grenade drops in the trench. I immediately let fly the Mills I have in my hand and follow up with another, over the block. Tug springs to his feet and joins me. We send over another one apiece. There is no reply.

I look round to see what the Pole Cat is doing. He is still crouched against the trench wall, but his face is a mass of blood. I cross over to him, leaving Tug on guard. There is a hole in the Pole Cat's head about the size of a half-crown, from which brain and blood are oozing. It does not need a second glance to tell me he has eaten his last piece of chocolate. Already the flies are beginning to settle on him. I find an empty sandbag close at hand and cover his face with it.

About an hour later Taters comes up. I report what has happened. He tells us we are going to be relieved, and sure enough in less than half hour our bombing post is taken over from us by a corporal and three men of a famous Scotch battalion.

A few hours later we are in billets near Villers-au-Bois. While here we learn fully what had happened to us on the ridge. Jerry had massed all the guns he could and put down on us a hellish barrage that had completely destroyed the front line, and had isolated us by a box barrage, (that is a continued curtain of fire on both flanks, to prevent any reinforcements coming to our support).

Our division lost so heavily in this attack that we are ordered out of the line for a month to get up to strength again. We are going back tomorrow to a mining village called Bruary about twelve miles behind the line.

"There is a hole in the "Pole-cats" head about the size of a half-crown, from which brain and blood are oozing. It does not need a second glance to tell me he has eaten his last piece of chocolate. ...... already the flies are beginning to settle on him ...... I find an empty sand-bag close at hand and cover his face with it ....

Reflection No 3
ON THE SOMME

September 5th 1916

We are in billets at the village of Franvillers, about eight kilometres (that is roughly about five miles) from the town of Albert. Our platoon has just been warned to parade at the armourer sergeant's for the purpose of having our bayonets sharpened. We have been in this billet for a week now, having left the Souchez sector in July and marching by stages to the Somme.

We can hear the continued rumble of the guns as the bombardment of the German positions around Mametz Wood prepares the way for the coming infantry attack. There is almost a continual procession of ambulances passing through on the way to the casualty clearing station. There must be an enormous amount of casualties.

Tug Wilson and I, having returned from having our toasting fork sharpened, are sitting outside the barn which serves as our billet. Tug is speaking about leave. "I should be on the next lot, Jimmy. D'yer think it'll be stopped agin? Gor blimey, I bet it's a bleedin' 'ot shop up there". His gaze wandered in the direction of the line. "Talk about Loos and Vimy and Festubert, I reckon they must 'er been a cake walk 'ter wot we got comin' to us up there". He paused to light an issue fag. "Let's come over ter the 'stamingy Jimmy, an' 'ave a drink. I got abart three francs left".

We put on our belt and side arms and proceed in the direction of the local estaminet. It is almost crowded with men of our battalion. Someone is banging out a tune on a very ancient and tinny piano, to accompany another who is singing a song which tells all and sundry that "Oh! Oh! Oh! It's a lovely war".

I push my way to the counter and order two beers. It is a lovely beverage, this beer. It tastes something like water in which lemon peel has been soaked. You couldn't get merry if you were to drink the River Somme full of it. They charge one penny a glass for it. It is not worth a penny a gallon. We finish our drinks quickly.

Tug goes over to the counter and attracts the attention of the stout lady who is the proprietor. "Madame ave-vou any rum? This beer of yours gives me a pain in the guts". Madam gives him a keen glance. "Rhom, messieur? Mais oui, I have ze cognac".

Tug put two francs on the counter. "Giv us two seprit francs worth, Ma. Ah, that's better. Better. Bit er guts in this, Jimmy. 'Ow the 'ell some blokes can sit guzzling that bleedin' French beer, I don't know. When I think of the luvly glass of Burton we used ter get for free 'apence before this war started, it almost makes me cry.

"An' d'yer remember too, dahn at Dirty Dick's in Shoreditch, free-pennoth of Irish 'ot wiv a bit of lemon in it? Or a pint of Burton wiv free-a-porth of rum in it? Ah, they was a man's drink they was. Gor blimey, for a couple of bob you could get blindo and go home in a cab.

"Wot about anuvver drop er con-e-ac? Jimmy, give us a franc. I've only got a franc left…'Ere Marie – oncore two

29

con-e-ags. Merci. Good luck Jimmy. Wish I had some money, I'd 'ave a gut full of this ter night. Tain't bad stuff. Almost as good as Blighty rum. Hullo, 'ere's old Jimmy Hurst. Wotcher Jimmy, 'ow goes it? 'Ow yer fixed? I can't treat yer, I'm napoo".

Taking this as my cue, I call for three cognacs. Jimmy Hurst is bubbling over with excitement. "Wot d'yer think? I just had the wire from old Taters. There's four men going on leave termorrow, an I'm one of 'em".

Tug finished his drink with a gulp. "Oo – you lucky basterd".

Jimmy Hurst gave him a hefty smack on the back. "Don't get excited Tug, you're anuvver".

I'm anuvver wot?"

"Why, you're anuvver, you're one of the four wot's goin' on leave. 'Ere, let's ave another drink. Three con-e-acks Marie. Cheerio. Why Tug, in anuvver couple of nights we'll be havin' a drink at the King's Arms".

"Is it straight away?" asked Tug. "Is it gospel? You ain't leadin' me up the garden?"

"Corse it's true. You take it from me, Tug. We're fer Blighty orlright termorrow, you'll see".

Tug applied a match to another issue fag. "Wot a time we'll 'ave, Jimmy. Fancy 'avin' a kip in a real bed agin. An breakfast in bed on Sunday morning. An readin' all about the bleedin war in the News of the World. I wonder if that barmaid's still dahn at the King's Arms? You know Jimmy, the ginger tart. Blimey, she wos 'ot stuff orlright".

"Well come along boys" I interrupted. "Let's get back to the billet, an' perhaps you'll hear something official about your leave. Besides I'm broke, so we can't have any more cognac." We finished up our drinks and made our way back to the barn.

At roll call that night Tug and Jimmy Hurst were warned to proceed on leave the following morning. I was warned for headquarters guard.

September 12th 1916

We have moved further up towards the line and are now in dugouts in the Mametz Wood. It hardly resembles a wood now, being but a collection of tree stumps, shell holes, blown-in dugouts, barbed wire, bully beef tins, battered shrapnel helmets, and pieces of equipment of all sorts.

Here and there legs and arms protrude from the earth. Just outside my dugout a leg is sticking out from a shell hole. A leg complete with puttees and spur, evidently the leg of some artilleryman.

Big shells are bursting with monotonous regularity on our vicinity and we have had several casualties since arriving in the wood. The bombardment seems as if it will never end. A little distance to our rear is a dressing station at which a continual stream of walking wounded is arriving.

Salvage parties are searching the wood for discarded rifles, ammunition and equipment. I am one of a party detailed at dusk to take up Mills bombs and ammunition to the front line.

Sep 12TH 1916

We have moved further up towards the line and are now in dug-outs in the Mametz wood. It hardly resembles a wood now being but a collection of tree stumps - shell holes - blown in dug outs - barbed wire - bully beef tins - battered shrapnel helmets, and pieces of equipment of all sorts - Here and there legs and arms protrude from the earth.

September 15th 1916
The High Woods (Flers)

It is not yet dawn. In about five minutes the signal will be given and we shall be out of the trench and over the top and facing what is coming to us. We know who are opposite us in the German trenches. Raiding parties have returned with proof that the line is held by the famous Third Bavarian Division.

Our artillery is putting down a barrage on their trenches such as I have never witnessed before. It seems impossible that anything could live under it.

Red lights are going up in dozens in the German lines, calling for more artillery support, and in answer comes their barrage.

Three minutes to go now.

Men are being killed and wounded from high explosive and shrapnel, as the enemy shells burst almost on our parapet. My thoughts turn to Jimmy Hurst and Tug Wilson, home on leave in Blighty, about them reading about the war in the News of the World on Sunday. Ah! they were lucky. They had escaped this lot alright.

Two minutes to go.

A man pitches forward almost on top of me, blood gushing from his mouth. Young Varnall, poor little cuss, hardly eighteen yet.

One minute.

"Get ready boys. Everything all correct? Mills Bombs! Steady..." The loud blast of the platoon officer's whistle. Clambering up on to the parapet. Over you go.

Rat-tat-tat-tat...Rat-tat-tat-tat...Machine gun bullets spraying the parapet. Men falling headlong into the trench. Get on. On. Damn the wire. I'm caught.

Who's that gone down? Sergeant Tattersall. Poor old Taters. Don't stop! Leave him alone. Get on! Rat-tat-tat-tat...God, they're going down in heaps. Look! Over there – the tanks. So it was true, all those rumours...

"Come on boys! Keep close up behind the tanks!"

I fall head-first into a trench. I'm hit. Germans cowering at the entrance of a dug-out. Blood streaming down my face, over my equipment.

Lieutenant Wiley, with the sleeve of his tunic saturated with blood. "You're wounded. Get back and take some of these blasted Jerries with you".

"Come on Jerry, come back with me".

"Kamerad! You are blessé (wounded). Let me bind your face up".

"Come on, no time for that now! Get out! Come on, allez! Get a move on!"

Back! Over the torn-up ground, get back! If you can – every yard a death trap. "Drop down in this shell hole for a while, you Jerries. Now put this bandage round my face". Plenty of blood but I don't think it's too bad. That's better. "Come on, let's make another spurt. Come on, what's up with you Fritz?" Christ, he's a stiff 'un.

On again. Our front line trench at last. Now the communications trench. Notice boards. "Walking wounded this way". Battalion headquarters.

"Stop here, you Jerries. Someone will see to you in a minute. I'm off to the dressing station".

September 16th 1916
The Rest Camp

I am unlucky. I am not being sent to Blighty, but instead have been sent to the rest camp at Franvillers. I have been before the M.O. and he says my wound will be alright again in a fortnight or so. He has taken a small piece of shrapnel from my right cheek and told me to see him each morning.

The rest camp is a new stunt to receive all the most lightly wounded cases, and thus avoid congestion at the base hospitals where the more badly wounded go prior to being sent to Blighty. It is a collection of tents in what was once an orchard. There is nothing to do except to sit about, play cards, mope, or write letters home. It is like being in an internment camp.

All sorts of cases are here, from lightly wounded to boils on the neck. One tent is full of men suspected of having dysentery, and each time they visit the latrine they have to report the fact to an orderly of the R.A.M.C. who is stationed near there. He makes a note of the man's name and on the next visit to the M.O. the number of visits to the latrine is stated.

Some of the dysentery cases get sent to the base hospital. A good many are simply swinging the lead with the object of keeping out of the line as long as possible. Who can blame them for that? No sane man who has had one taste of the Somme is ever in a hurry to get back to it again. Those "heroes" who are "bursting" to get back again at the enemy exist only in the minds of old ladies, armchair critics at home and novelette writers.

Sometimes the M.O. asks a dysentery case for a sample of his stool. I have known some of these dysentery cases who have not had a motion of their bowels for several days, but dare not ask the M.O. for an aperient as they are supposed to be continually visiting the latrine. They had to go through the motion of visiting the latrine in order to have their visits recorded by the orderly.

Some of these have even borrowed a sample of stool from a man who really did have a touch of dysentery, and after examination of this the M.O. has sent them to the base hospital, from whence, if they have been good swingers, they have been sent to that haven of all soldiers – Blighty.

There is only one thing you get plenty of in this camp, and that is rest. So much of it, in fact, that after a few days of it you get bored to death. No recreation apart from perhaps a game of cards, no money, and two packets of cigarettes (issue gaspers) once a week. The only parade is the visit to the M.O. each morning and the usual question "How are you? Any aches or pains?"

Some men, in order to get a few more days respite from the line, complain of their eyes in order to pay a visit to the eye specialist to get glasses. Some, who are already in possession of artificial teeth, tell a tale of losing them in action.

But the M.O. is wise to most of these tricks, and every morning sees a large party detailed and equipped ready to return to their regiments. To take another chance in that gamble of life and death, where the odds are always heavy against the poor infantryman…the bloodbath of the Somme.

September 25th 1916
Return to the Line

I have paid my last visit to the M.O. at the rest camp. He has told me I am quite fit and has warned me to report to the sergeant major to draw equipment in order to return to my unit.

So at 9.30am I, with about twenty other men of various regiments, set off on our journey back to the line.

Each of us have a day's ration in our haversack. I am the only one of my battalion, the others belonging to other battalions of the division.

Off we start through the village of Franvillers, in the charge of a lance corporal who is also returning to duty. It is raining. We are <u>not</u> "all merry and bright". Far from it – not one of us is bursting to get back at the "Beastly Boche". As far as my experience goes, the only persons who are bursting to get back at Jerry are those who have never seen him, and are never likely to.

We look longingly at the estaminet as we pass it. We are not likely to see another on this side of the wilderness we are making for. Ambulances dash by with their loads of wounded. The same thought is in each man's mind. Sooner be in one of them with a wound of some sort, going to the comfort of a clean bed in the base hospital. And after that, Blighty, and perhaps no more of this ghastly existence of mud, lice, anxiety and torture.

On we go, through the town of Albert, with its hanging virgin. Towards night we pass through Fricourt and the corporal calls a halt and tells us to find a dugout in which to spend the night. The rain is still teeming down. The battered trenches and dugouts, rusty barbed wire and stunted tree trunks are a scene to strike despair and desolation to the heart.

Let us find a hole to crawl into, where perhaps we can find oblivion for a few hours in sleep. Let's try this one. Slithering down the muddy slimy steps we reach the bottom.

Someone produces a candle. What's that heap in the corner? No need to ask that question. The smell will tell you that it's a dead Jerry. Let's find another hotel, this one don't seem healthy.

Up the steps again, stumbling and sliding. Here's another one, try this. Ah, no one at home – alive or dead! This'll do us. Now for a bit of bully beef and biscuit. If we could only boil a mess tin of water we could make some tea. But there is nothing we can burn, so that is out of the question. Let's finish up our bully and biscuits and then have a kip.

I take stock of my companions. The lance corporal of the 8th Londons is a man about thirty-five. Another in the same battalion is a lad who looks about eighteen. And two more of the 7th Battalion, both youngsters about twenty. The others of our party are in other dugouts in the vicinity. We settle down. The lance corporal blows out the candle.

I try to sleep. Something heavy runs across my face. A rat. I strike a match and light a gasper. The lice are getting busy and are biting like hell. I am dead tired but cannot sleep. The others are already snoring. This won't do. I must shut it out somehow. I finish my fag and shut my eyes. Another rat runs across my chest. It feels as heavy as a cat. These rats must be living well in these parts.

At last I doze off and seem to have slept for about an hour when I am awakened by the lance corporal who says it is six o'clock and time we got a move on. We stretch our limbs and stumble out of the dugout.

Reflection No 4

IN THE YPRES SALIENT

January 5th 1917

We are in the line holding trenches in front of Ypres near the famous Hill 60. The trenches are no longer knee-deep in water, for the intense cold has frozen every drop of moisture and we stand, and slip about, on solid ice. The greatcoats of the sentries as they stand at their posts on the fire steps are frozen stiff as boards. In the shelters or funk holes a brazier with a coke fire provides a little warmth for those not actually on duty.

Such intense cold as the winter of 1916-1917 produced had not been experienced for many years. All the world seems white. At night, raiding parties go out covered all up in a white smock and shrapnel helmets coated with whitewash, making them invisible against the white background of No Man's Land.

Most of the men in the platoon are newcomers from England, a good percentage being conscripts. Gone are the lads of the Loos, Vimy Ridge and Somme days. Never more will I see Sergeant Tattersall, more widely known as Taters. Young Varnall, the poor little eighteen years old boy who should never have left England. Corporal Jackson and the Pole Cat, killed at Vimy. Jimmy Hurst, killed on his first journey to the line after returning from leave. Tug Wilson, killed by a rifle grenade near Flers (also his first time in the line after returning from leave).

Yes, nearly all new faces in the platoon now. One or two old ones remain. Corporal (now Sergeant) Hulland, who is now the platoon sergeant, Lance Corporal Meen, Ted Castell and one or two more. We have a platoon officer newly arrived from England, Lieutenant Dane. Also a new company officer, Captain Adams, and a new company sergeant major, Philpots.

The spirit of youthfulness seems to have departed and to have been swallowed up in the shambles of the Somme. A good percentage of the men are married and in the late thirties. Good enough soldiers in their way, but lacking the boyish enthusiasm of the lads of 1914 and 1915. But then, what would you expect? These men have responsibilities unknown to the earlier lads. Wives, businesses to study. And so they come up with their Derby Group or later come as conscripts.

We do four days in the line, four days in reserve dugouts at the Chateau Belge and four days back in a collection of semi-circular huts known as Halifax Camp.

During the four days at this camp we have the luxury of a bath and change of underclothing. Our dirty, lice-infested shirts and pants are taken away and we are given clean ones in exchange. But alas they are clean only in theory, for they are lined with lice eggs and ere another twenty four hours has passed we are as lousy as ever.

Each of our huts has to accommodate about twenty four men, and it is a work of art to settle down at night for sleep. But the main thing is to get warm and we manage this alright in the crowded hut.

Anything is better than being in the line this bitter weather, but the four days soon slip by and up we go for another four days in front of Hill 60.

Continual mining is going on in this sector and a large tunnel running from the front line to the support line is capable of holding a large number of men. The company holding the front line has one of its platoons in support in the tunnel on consecutive days, thus providing a day out of the line for each of the four platoons. This day is mostly passed in assisting the sappers and miners by removing the excavated earth in sandbags.

It was on one of our platoon visits to the tunnel that being rather thirsty, and having no water in my bottle at the time, I asked my mate Ted Castell to oblige me with a drink.

Taking his bottle out of the holder, he handed it to me. I had a good swig and nearly choked – it was full of rum. Ted had been on the scrounge and "won" it from somewhere, for Ted was a champion scrounger.

We found a quiet corner and proceeded to cane that water-bottle of rum, which we did to such an extent that I had no further recollection of anything until I was awakened by someone kicking me in the back at Stand To next morning.

We are being relieved again and are going back to Halifax Camp instead of doing our four days in reserve at the Chateau Belge. There are rumours of something special being afoot. Rumours that later on we find are, by way of a change, correct.

The Rehearsal

We have left Halifax Camp and have gone further back to billets at Dickebusch Huts. The second day we are here we are informed by our company officer that we are out of the line for several days to prepare for a raid on the German trenches near the Bluff by Hill 60.

The whole scheme is outlined to us. Each man is to thoroughly rehearse his part. Trenches are to be dug to resemble the German position at the bluff, which has been photographed by the R.F.C. Every machine gun, every trench mortar position and dugout is mapped out. Each platoon has its special job.

The company officer is quite enthusiastic about it. "It is a great honour for our battalion to be picked for this stunt", he tells us. "Each man of you will have a thorough training in his part. And at the end of this rehearsal we simply go in the line, make the raid, do as much damage as we can, smash up trench mortars, machine guns etc. and bring back as many prisoners as possible. And then we come straight out of the line and have a good time at Poperinghe". His glance roved over the entire company. "Tell me, is there anyone in the company who is not keen on this stunt?"

No one answered. Everyone, then, was apparently keen on this adventure. What was the use of saying otherwise? Woe betide the man who said he was not keen on it, but they could not stop each man from having his own ideas about the affair.

A great honour to be picked for this stunt? Oh yes! Fine stunt, to go over in broad daylight to smash up the formidable German position at the Bluff. It was going to be no cake walk, and some of us would not come back to have that good time at Poperinghe.

But what was the use of thinking about things like that? It did not do to look too far ahead in those days. Anyway, we are out of the line for a fortnight at least and we are going to have extra rations too, and all we've got to do is play at mimic warfare.

We shall be sure of a warm kip every night, and that is something to look forward to in these bitter cold nights, so perhaps we are lucky after all? The worst that can happen to one is to stop a full packet and push up the daisies, or one might be lucky and stop a cushy Blighty. If one comes back untouched then there is the good time at Pop – probably a concert, a few days rest and de-lousing parade.

There is not much civilian life in the vicinity of our huts. An estaminet and a few farmhouses where one can buy, for a franc, "deux oeufs, pommes de terre du pain and café au lait". Or in plain Cockney language two fried eggs, fried chips in a roll and a cup of coffee. Not a bad little feed for a franc, which is about tenpence.

In the morning too, at reveille, we can get "un petit verre de café et cognac" (a small glass of coffee and cognac) for fourpence, and this is a fine drink to buck you up on a cold morning. So for the time being we shall be in clover compared with the others who are doing their four in and four out.

We have been at the huts now for ten days rehearsing our jobs until every man is now certain of his particular job. Our company has to penetrate the German front line and smash up everything we can. The other companies are to enter the enemy's support and reserve trenches and do likewise. On a given signal the whole will return, bringing with them as many prisoners and machine guns as possible.

In two days' time we shall go up the line and make the raid. Several lead swingers, who do not relish the idea of the raid have developed various complaints and gone sick, but the M.O. is up to all their dodges and only a few genuine cases have been sent to hospital.

One member of our platoon, Dicky Saville, a married man of about forty years of age, is in sore trouble. He has received news from home that his wife is dangerously ill and has told his trouble to the company officer. He has been informed that after the raid he may be allowed to go on leave, but that nothing can be done before. He has never been over the top before, and is full of melancholy forebodings. We try to cheer him up, but without success.

Meanwhile we are still living like fighting cocks. Double rations and plenty of sleep, which seems to me something like fattening up the turkey for Christmas.

We had a concert last night in a large barn. A makeshift stage was fixed and several good turns were given by members of the battalion concert party. One item on the programme, however, did not go seem to down very well. This was a chap who sang in a baritone voice "Trumpeter, trumpeter, what are you sounding now?" Not very tactful, I thought, in view of the fact of what we were going up for shortly, especially when he came to that part "They're lying around with their faces to the ground, and they can't hear me calling reveille".

But perhaps he was only trying to cheer us up. Anyway, he wasn't going to be in the raid himself (all the concert party members would be sent to the transport lines) so perhaps his thoughts were different to ours.

Feb 20th 1917
The Raid on the Bluff

We are in the line in front of the Bluff. We came in last night and relieved the other battalion in our brigade who had been holding the line. They filed out of the trenches with many wishes for our welfare and hopes "that we'd have a good time".

Some looked at us with a sort of awe, as one would look at a man who was going to swallow poison. One asked, as he passed me in the crowded trench, "Blimey mate, are you reely goin' over the top 'ere?" I informed him such was the case. He passed on with a muttered "Gor Blimey! You ain't 'arf askin' for it, you bleedin' Cast Irons". (Cast Iron Sixth was the nickname of our battalion).

It is ten minutes to five. We are all lined up on the parapet, bayonets fixed, ready to go over at five. The platoon sergeant comes round with a mess tin of rum, dishing out two tablespoonsful to each man. Some of the men decline their share, so that after making his round he finds he has still some buckshee rum left. So I come in for another big tot and the sergeant knocks back the remainder. It is not a case of:

> If the sergeant drinks your rum never mind
> If the sergeant drinks your rum don't cuss and blind
> He's entitled to a tot
> But not the bleedin' lot
> So if the sergeant drinks your rum nev-er mind

Every man had his share if he wanted it, so there was no harm in the sergeant knocking back what was left.

I was feeling quite comfortable with my big issue of rum inside my belly when the two minutes bombardment of the German positions begins. A mine is blown up in the enemy trenches on our left. This is done as a feint to draw the German guns who send over shrapnel on our trench. Almost at my side a man is killed. It is Dicky Saville, so the question of his going on leave is settled. Perhaps he would see his wife again, over the great divide…

The whistle blows. Over we go!

Almost before we know it we are in the German front line – our objective. Here we must stop until the withdraw signal is given. We commence to carry out our instructions, bombing dugouts and generally doing as much damage as possible.

Many Jerries are lying dead and wounded in the trench. Others are holding their hands up and crying "Kamerad!" I am talking to one of them when a bomb is thrown from behind a traverse and I am wounded in the leg. Ted Castell rips my puttee and trouser leg open and binds up the wound, which is just below my left knee.

I crawl into a dugout which is occupied by three Germans who have already shown their readiness to surrender. We have got to stop here until the signal to withdraw sounds, so I make myself as comfortable as possible.

One of the Jerries offers me a cigarette. Another lights it for me. The other, in broken English, asks me if my wound is very bad. They seem dazed by this sudden daylight raid and are doing their best to be friendly. The one who enquired about my wound says "Ve are gompletely subrised dot you kom on so queek. Bud nefer mind, ve are prisoner aindt it? Goot! All de better. I am of dees war vot you call it fed up. Anytink must be better dan dees tefil of a war. I am glat I am finish. You are de Londons regiment aind't it? Goot. I haf peen in London pefore dees war pegin. Ah, dose vos de peutiful days! You tink dey sent us to London? Yes?"

Ted Castell enters with two more prisoners. "Hullo Jimmy! How yer feeling? Here's another couple of birds for the cage when we get back! How's yer legs feeling?" He hands me his water-bottle. "Take a swig of this. You know what it is. Drop of daddy's comfort".

I take a good swig of the rum and the blood courses through my veins and I feel warm all over. Wonderful stuff this Army rum. More wonderful still is how Ted Castell always seems to be in possession of a water bottle full of it, but that's Ted's secret. But he sure is the champion scrounger.

The German artillery has now begun to shell our trenches in earnest. We shall have a rough passage going back. I go to the entrance of the dugout and look out over the German lines. Red lights are going up in their reserve trenches. Evidently the boys are enjoying themselves there alright.

Our platoon sergeant enters the dugout. He is wounded in the arm, which is roughly bandaged. Ted hands him the water bottle and he takes a swig at it.

"Ah! That's good. Well boys, we look like having a hot time getting back. Some of our boys have gone west. Young Vickers, poor old Stokes, Corporal Smith, Dickson....all napoo. Wonder how the other companies are getting on in the support and reserve trenches? How many Jerries you got here? Five? Well give 'em a tot each of your rum, Ted. I expect the poor blighters can do with it. Won't be long now before the signal comes to go back. Ah, there it goes! Come on boys. Come on you square-heads, get a move on. Get back as quick as you can. Can you manage alright with that leg, Jimmy? Right, come on".

Out of the dugout we go. Over the bashed-in parapet. Out into No Man's Land, dodging the shell holes and the German shrapnel shells which are coming over pretty thick. Tumbling into our own front line trench, we hand our prisoners over to an escort which is waiting for them. Into a dug out where we get a big tot of rum and a smoke. The raid on the Bluff is over.

... We commence to carry out our instructions ... bombing dug-outs ... and generally doing as much damage as possible ... Many 'Jerries' are lying dead and wounded in the trench ... others are holding their hands up and crying "Kamerad" I am talking to one of them when a bomb is thrown from behind a traverse and I am wounded in the leg. Ted Castell rips my puttee and trouser leg open and binds up the wound which is just below my left knee. I crawl into a dug-out which is occupied by three Germans who have already shown their

90

Reflection No. 5

3rd BATTLE OF YPRES

MESSINES RIDGE

June 3rd 1917

I did not get to Blighty with the wound I received in the raid on the Bluff on February 20th. I got as far as the base hospital at Boulogne where I stayed for a few weeks and spent another month at the convalescent camp there.

I have had one turn in the trenches facing the Messines Ridge and we are now in bivouac a few miles behind the line. There is a big battle coming off, that is obvious to everybody. Troops are everywhere – in huts, tents, bivouac and billets. Great ammunition dumps are scattered over the area. Overhead the Royal Flying Corps are busy, bombing and taking photographs of the German lines, and our artillery maintain a ceaseless bombardment of the enemy trenches.

We have been told we are to attack the Messines Ridge and we have just completed a three weeks training some miles behind the line, in preparation. We do not know the exact date of the attack but we know it will be very soon. It will be the biggest battle of the war, up to date. Mines have been dug under the German positions, and before the battle begins it is expected that the German trenches will be blown sky-high.

It is evident that Jerry knows of the coming storm, for he keeps up a stiff bombardment of our communications. Last night he blew up one of our ammunition dumps, and it was like a Crystal Palace firework display.

Ted Castell has been promoted. He is now a lance corporal, but he doesn't seem over keen on being a N.C.O. In his own words "They arst me to take the stripe, Jimmy. I'd sooner be wiv'art it. Wen yer've got a stripe yer carn't mix up wiv yer mates like yer want to. Never mind, spose I'll git used to it in time". Ted is a bit of a nut. I asked him once what he was in peace time. He looked at me and grinned. "Well if yer wants ter know Jimmy, I don't mind telling yer. I'm a burglar". Whether he was pulling my leg I don't know, but he certainly knew how to get a water bottle of rum now and then.

June 6ᵗʰ 1917

We are going up into the line in readiness for the attack on Messines Ridge. Loaded up with bombs, shovels, wire-cutters, sandbags, extra bandoliers of ammunition etc., we leave our bivouac and make our way across country, skirting the ghostly, tortured city of Ypres. Passing on the way many results of the German bombardment of our communications. Smashed motor lorries, mutilated horses and pack mules, overturned ambulances and wrecked artillery limbers and guns. Fresh shell holes all along the road. Here and there a dead man hastily dragged to the side of the road and covered with a ground sheet.

The men are silent mostly, as they move towards the line. They do not sing "It's a long, long, way to Tipperary" as some writers would have you believe. Anyhow, they would not be allowed to sing if they felt so inclined. Silence is the order. Silence, and no smoking.

It may be a "long, long, way to Tipperary" but it's not very far to the trenches in front of the Messines Ridge. And each man is rather serious, for this time tomorrow night he knows not where he may be. He may still be safe and sound, he may be badly wounded, he may be on his way to England with a cushy Blighty one, or he may be lying out in that shell-bashed hell of desolation awaiting the attention of the burial party.

I would like some of those writers who are so fond of describing in their narratives how the men "went singing and cracking jokes into the line, anxious only to get at grips once again with the beastly Bosche", to take their place in the platoon tonight as an ordinary rifleman going into the line on the eve of a battle, the like of which has never occurred before in the history of war. I think they would then be cured forever of writing such trash.

Heroes do not go into action singing patriotic songs. The true hero is the man who is secretly afraid of what he is going into, but can put his fear into the background and carry on.

Ted Castell is marching next to me. "Wot's the matter Jimmy?" he asks in low tones. "Wot yer finking abaht? Cheer up! We'll be orlright. Yer know wot the captin told us. It's goin' ter be a bleedin' walkover for us. The mines are goin' orf and they're goin' ter blow the Jerries ter 'ell. If there's any left arter the mines go orf, the artillery is gonna see 'em orf. All we gotter do is ter walk through. Yus, like takin' a stroll fru Victoria Park on Sunday mornin', that's all – I don't fink".

"That's right, Ted" I answer. "They always tell the same old fairy tale. It's always going to be a cake walk. It was the same yarn at Loos and the Somme. We know better! But never mind, let's hope for the best. We may get a trip to Blighty out of this stunt".

7th June 1917

We are in the trenches in front of the Messines Ridge. It is three o'clock in the morning and everything seems extraordinary quiet, the lull before the storm.

Our platoon spent about two hours during the night cutting the wire in front of the support trench, so that we can have a clear passage when we go over. We are going over from the support trench, following the attacking wave at present in the front line. Verey Lights are going up in large quantities in the German lines and everything looks weird and ghostly in the eerie light of the coming dawn. In front of us looms the sinister Hill 60, scene of many a desperate encounter.

We have just had our issue of rum. The platoon officer has given us our final instructions. In ten minutes, hell will be let loose on such a scale never yet attempted. We are all ready, bayonets fixed, bombs ready for immediate use. This is always the worst part of the business, waiting to go over.

Waiting.

Jerry is sending a few shrapnel shells over.

Five minutes to go...

Ten minutes past three...

And then with a crash like the last crack of doom the mines were exploded.

The support trench in which we crouched waiting rocked like a ship at sea. Through clouds of smoke and flying debris, barbed wire posts, uprooted tree stumps, fragments of what were once living men, we can see the summit of Hill 60 enveloped in one great orange flame. Simultaneously the long lines of our artillery, field batteries, howitzers and heavies belched forth their contribution to the inferno.

And then we went over.

At the last minute we are directed to go by way of the communication trench until we reach our front line. At the junction of the communication trench and our front line we stumble on a ghastly sight .The parapet is levelled, and dead and wounded men are lying about in every conceivable attitude.

We pick our way over the dead. One man I noticed was kneeling on one knee as if in an attitude of prayer, stone dead. Another dead man was against the broken parapet, reclining as if asleep. Under a pile of debris legs and arms are protruding.

German shells are dropping thick and heavy as we push on until we reach what remains of the enemy front line where groups of dazed and trembling Germans are holding their hands up imploring pity and mercy. Shattered and completely demoralised, they gladly make their way to our lines.

Now the German guns turn on us with increased volume, killing and wounding friend and foe alike. Such an inferno I never thought could be possible. It seems incredible that anything could live in this hell of destruction.

Isolated German machine guns open fire on us and several of our platoon go down, among them Ted Castell who gets a bullet through his thigh. I am just bending over him to bandage him up when there is a blinding flash and I am lifted off my feet and crashed down on top of poor old Ted.

I stagger to my feet. My left hand feels numb. I see it is smothered in blood. I rip out my field dressing and roughly bandage it, then I take another look at Ted. He is lying very quiet, blood oozing from his forehead. He has received another wound. I take out his dressing and fix his head up as well as I can, while another man in the platoon binds up his leg.

There is nothing else now I can do for Ted. He will have to wait until the stretcher bearers come along, so I turn away and make my way back to our lines.

Soon I am one of a long procession of walking wounded, and through the communication trench we go until we reach the advance dressing station. Here a crowd of walking wounded is sitting about outside the entrance of the dugout.

After about a hour my turn comes to go in. Our battalion chaplain is in there assisting the M.O. He is bending over a man on a stretcher as I enter. The man is moaning and begging for a drink of water.

The M.O. bends over him and does something to his arm with a kind of needle. The man ceases his moaning and lies quiet.

The chaplain approaches me. "Where are you wounded, my son?"

"In the hand".

"Ah! You are indeed fortunate to come out of that inferno with nothing more serious. Give thanks to God who watched over you. This poor boy here" (he pointed to the man who had been moaning for water and who now lay with closed eyes, and on whose face the hue of death was approaching). "This poor lad, we could not even give him the drink of water he craved for. He has been shot through the stomach".

After my wound had been more comfortably dressed, I was put into an ambulance and away we went to the casualty clearing station. Here we stayed but a few hours and then boarded a hospital train which took us to Havre. Here we were kept in hospital for a couple of days and then embarked on a hospital ship.

Next morning we arrived at Southampton and l was sent to hospital at Eastleigh a few miles distant. Blighty at last, after an absence of eighteen months. How good it seems to see English women and girls and English shops. How grand to be out of the sound of gunfire. Peace. It is good to be alive in England on this beautiful June day.

Reflection No. 6

BLIGHTY

THE RESERVE BATTALION

August 1917

After six weeks in hospital and ten days sick leave (which I overstayed by four days) I reported for duty at the reserve battalion at Deepcut (Blackdown Camp) near Aldershot. On arrival I was promptly bunged into the clink.

The following morning I appeared before the company officer and was awarded seven days C.B. While serving my seven days confinement to barracks I reported sick (having lost my false teeth during the action at Messines Ridge). I was sent to the garrison dentist who took an impression of my gums and told me to report to him in a week's time.

A few days later I was warned that I was in the next draft for France and I was to proceed the following day on six days draft leave. I reported again to the dentist and told him I was on a draft for France. He was quite indignant about it. "You will not be fit for a draft unless I say you are fit. You are under my care while you are awaiting dentures. But anyway, you take your six days draft leave and see me again as soon as you return. Understand?" And his right eye closed in a beautiful wink.

I proceeded on my leave. Almost every night I was at home there was an air raid. Maroons sounding "Take cover! Take cover!" Women running with babies in their arms to tube stations or any sort of place that seemed to promise shelter.

On my return to Blackdown I reported to the dentist. He told me to take no notice but to fall in with the draft on the day of departure for France. A few days after we were told we were proceeding to France the following morning.

Next morning the orderly sergeant was shouting "Fall in the draft!" On the parade ground we fell in, about a hundred of us. After a while along comes the Colonel. Tell us what a fine body of men we were, and said he was sure we would keep up the traditions of the battalion when we reached the famous battalion which had so distinguished itself in the glorious battles of Loos, Festubert, the Somme, Messines Ridge etc. He then handed each one of us a pipe and a tobacco pouch, and of course shook each one of us by the hand and wished us the best of luck.

The orderly sergeant then called us to attention and shouted "Draft! Num-ber. Form fours. Left, right turn! Fall out on the right the following men: Cope, James, Russel". And then stepped up to the Colonel, saluted and said "Three men unfit, Sir. Three waiting men have taken their place. Already to move off now, Sir?"

Then the Colonel gave the order "Draft, form fours. Right by the left. Quick march!" The band struck up and off they went to the station. I was left behind with my pipe and pouch.

A visit to the Glass House

A few weeks after I had been declared unfit for the draft I was again warned for France. I was now in possession of my dentures, so of course I should not be unfit this time. I was given another six days draft leave.

I returned four days over my time, with the usual result – guard room, company office next morning. I was ordered to be confined to barracks until the day of departure for France.

About a week later orders were posted up that the drafts of the various battalions in Blackdown under orders for France would be inspected the following afternoon at two o'clock by the general officer commanding the district.

At about one o'clock (that is an hour before the inspection) I, with two more men of the draft by the names of Wright and Clark, suddenly decided we could not be bothered by the spit and polish of a general's inspection, and thought we would have a few hours in London before going to France again.

Accordingly we made a big detour round the back of the camp, and keeping our eyes skinned for our mortal enemy, the Redcaps (military police) we reached Chertsey, and by means of old draft leave vouchers faked up to date, boarded a train to Waterloo, which however we left at Vauxhall in order to dodge the Redcaps who are numerous at Waterloo.

We spent the night in the home of Wright, whose father immediately on seeing us got the wind up to a great extent and insisted on us returning. So after an early breakfast (about four o'clock) he gave his son a pound note to pay our fares back and we departed. We caught the first train from Waterloo (about five o'clock) and arrived at Farnborough (about three miles from Blackdown) about half past six.

Just before we reached camp we heard sounds of martial music approaching near, so we dodged behind the hedge. As the band proceeded past our hiding place we perceived to our dismay that behind them were our draft, fully equipped. They were en route for the railway station, and France! Here was a fine how do you do. Clark wanted to fall in with them there and then. Wright and I had to hold him down.

After the procession had gone out of sight we continued on our way to Blackdown and reported ourselves at the orderly room. We were immediately escorted to the garrison clink and locked each in a separate cell.

The following morning an escort took us in front of the company officer, who read over the charge to us. "Breaking out of barracks, absenting yourself from general officer's parade and evading a draft for France whilst on active service. What have you to say?"

"We admit breaking out of barracks, but we had no intention of dodging the draft. Catching so early a train as five o'clock in the morning showed we wanted to be in time for the draft. We did not think the draft would depart so early".

"Remanded for commanding officer. Escort and prisoners – right turn, quick march".

Next morning. Outside the battalion orderly room with our escort, myself, Wright and Clark. Wright is the first to be marched. After an interval he is marched out again. Then Clark is marched in, and later out. Then comes my turn. Sergeant major shouts "Prisoner! Hat off! Escort and prisoner!! Quick march! Mark time! Halt!"

"Number 322019. Rifleman W.E. James. Breaking out of barracks. Absenting himself from general officer's parade. Evading a draft proceeding to France, whilst on active service. Anything to say?"

"I admit breaking out of barracks and being absent from general's parade. I did not wilfully avoid going with the draft. I was under the impression the draft would leave Blackdown much later than they did".

"Will you take my punishment, or do you prefer to be tried by court martial?"

"I will take your punishment, Sir".

"Twenty eight days detention".

"Escort and prisoner! Right turn. Quick march".

The next morning the three of us were escorted to the Aldershot detention barracks, known to soldiers by its nickname the glass house on account of its glass roof. I had the biggest sentence of the three, twenty eight days. Wright had fourteen days. Clark had ten days.

DRAFT OF THE 6ᵀᴴ LONDONS AT BLACKDOWN CAMP JUST BEFORE LEAVING FOR FRANCE. THROUGH MISSING THIS DRAFT I GOT TWENTY EIGHT DAYS DETENTION IN THE "GLASS HOUSE".

Reflection No. 7
PALESTINE

After finishing my twenty eight days in the glass house I was escorted back to camp and taken before the company officer, who informed me that I had been detailed to form one of a draft of about fifty men to proceed to Palestine and be attached to the second battalion of the Queen's Westminster Rifles.

I asked him if I could have a draft leave. I thought he was going to have a fit. "Well, you have got a nerve" he said, "asking for leave. You've had two leaves, and dodged both drafts. Anyway, I'll see what can be done. What sort of a time did you have in the detention barracks?"

I told him the food was better than it was at the camp, and that I was fairly comfortable during my term of detention, having been given a job as cleaner in the sergeants' mess. He dismissed me and I returned to the barrack room.

About three days after, we fell in for equipment and draft leave. Once again I was handed a draft leave warrant, this time with dreadful warnings as to what would be my fate if I failed to return at the proper time. Eventually I returned, four days over my time, and was bundled into the clink, where I remained until the draft, myself included this time, left for Palestine.

We first proceeded to Havre, and then by horse train to Marseilles and then embarked on the SS Karoa for Alexandria, Egypt. One night at the rest camp and then on to the infantry base depot at El-Kantara on the Suez Canal. About a fortnight there and then by train to Ludd, and after that marching by stages (bivouacking each night under little portable tents) through Enab, and passing Bethlehem on our left, up the hills where we joinded the Queen's Westminsters in the line outside Jerusalem.

Turkish Counter Attack on Jerusalem

Our draft had arrived, it seemed, at an opportune moment, as the Turks, who were very sore at the thoughts of losing possession of the Holy City, were bent on making a counter attack to try to regain it.

Hardly had we got into position when with blood curdling yells of "Allah! Al Allah! Allah Akabar!" the Turks were advancing to the attack. Our Lewis guns sung their song of death. Our rifles kept up a continuous rattle of rapid fire, and scores of Johnny Turks passed out by our bullets through the gates of Valallah, the Mohammedan paradise, there to receive the warrior's reward of everlasting joy, including ten thousand dark-eyed houris.

The counter-attack was repulsed and during the hours of darkness the main body of the enemy retreated, leaving only a small rear-guard on the hill, which was attacked and captured by one of our companies next morning.

Later on in the day we were relieved and went for a rest to an Arab village, from which we chased its lawful owners, who departed calling down upon us the vengeance of Allah upon the Christian dogs as they departed.

Holding the line in the Judean Hills

After the Turks had been driven from Jerusalem they retreated to Jericho, from which they were later on driven. They then retreated across the River Jordan and took up a position on the far bank. After a period of rest in a monastery on the Mount of Olives outside the Holy City, our battalion went into the line again, taking up a position in the Judean Hills.

Everything seemed peaceful, as indeed it might be, for Johnny Turk was miles away, with the plains of the Jordan between ourselves and him. At nights we could see the twinkling lights of his camp fires, but nothing disturbed us on our listening posts at night, save the weird howls of the jackals. In the daytime we retired to caves, of which there were plenty in the hills, leaving only a day O.P. (observation post) held by a couple of men.

The days were spent in various ways, such as catching the eternal lice, trying to wash a shirt (if one was fortunate enough to obtain enough water to do so, which was very rare), trying to make a pudding out of crushed up army biscuits and ration dates (and oh what lovely puddings they generally turned out). But they were always eaten whatever they looked or tasted like, for rations were none too plentiful in the Judean Hills.

Two tins of bully beef between three men, four army biscuits per man (and what biscuits they were, just like concrete). A handful of dates each, a tin of jam (and oh boy! what jam it was) between six men. About two ounces of cheese per man, and a water bottle filled, out of which we handed a pint of water to the company cook to provide us with our pint of tea – otherwise, no water to the cook meant no drink of tea.

On rare occasions we had a ration of bread instead of the biscuits. Sometimes we were able to buy bread (of a sort) from the Arabs, who charged us five piastres (about a shilling in English money) for a loaf of dirty-looking gritty bread, about the size of a teacake.

One result of this continual dry food and lack of green vegetables was that three quarters of the battalion broke out in sores and the medical officer always had a big sick parade. Sometimes we were issued out with lime juice as a remedy, and frequently we were dosed with quinine.

One day while I was on the sangar (post in the front line) the platoon sergeant asked me if I had any trade in civilian life. I told him I was a painter. He then asked me if I would like my name put down to go on a trade test. Not thinking I would hear more of it, I said yes.

Shortly after we were relieved and went into billets on the Mount of Olives outside Jerusalem. While here, I formed one of a guard over a water supply in the Garden of Gethsemane. What visions of the story of Christ's last hours it conjured up to me in the lonely hours of the night, as I took my turn at sentry at the water dump.

A few days later we went back into the line in the hills overlooking the Jordan plain. While here we were informed we were to take part in a raid – with the remainder of the division – on the Turkish position at Amman and Es-Salt, to destroy railheads and other places of importance.

The day came and we were all lined up, ready to move off, when I was warned by the company sergeant major to report at once to the transport lines, about four miles to the rear. I was at once the object of envy among my mates. I ventured to ask the S.M. if anything was wrong.

"Wrong?" he said. "Why you lucky swine, you're going to Cairo, and just as we're going into this stunt, too".

I was amazed. "Cairo!" I exclaimed. "What have I got to go to Cairo for?"

"On a blinkin' trade test", he said. "Off you go. Wish I was a painter".

And then I remembered having given my name in for a trade test, and it had come off too! So I reported to the R.S.M. at the transport lines and was to board any lorry at the dump in Jerusalem and proceed to the railhead at Ludd. On arrival at Ludd I reported to the R.T.O. and was given papers to proceed to El-Kantara, the infantry base depot on the Suez Canal.

On reaching here I spent the night and next morning had a lovely bath, a complete change of underclothing and a new outfit of khaki drill and solar topee (pith helmet complete with pugaree).

My next step was the Egyptian State Railway en route for Cairo. Here I reported and was sent to the Citadel Barracks near the Great Nile Bridge. I spent one night in the barracks, and oh! what a night it was, for the bugs in the bed were the biggest I had ever seen. And could they bite? Well, my body was smothered in blood from the bites. And then I understood why so few men slept in the great barrack room (which must have held at least fifty beds).

One of the few inmates of the rooms then enlightened me with the news that most men reporting at Cairo spent their nights at the Anzac Hotel run by the YMCA, where a clean bed and a good breakfast could be obtained for five piastres (about a shilling). So off to the Anzac I toddled and booked a bed for that night, and spent a comfortable night and had a good breakfast – a couple of eggs, bread and butter and tea – next morning, and all for a shilling.

At nine o'clock I reported at the Citadel Barracks to the master painter, who was an Italian. He asked me a few questions then gave me a wooden chair to sandpaper and apply a coat of paint. This took me about an hour, and I was told I was free to do as I liked until nine o'clock next morning. So off I went to the Anzac and booked a bed for the night.

I was now nearly broke, so I returned to the Citadel and in the canteen there I sold a razor and strop for ten piastres (two shilling and a penny). While drinking a pint someone remarked "There's a pay parade on outside, for blokes wots come dahn from the line". So outside I went and formed one of a line in front of an officer in the barrack square, seated at a small table. When my turn came I asked for – and got – five hundred piastres (about five guineas) and straight away made tracks for the Wazir (bazaar) feeling like Baron Rothschild.

Passing a beggar I gave him all the loose money I had on me (about two piastres) and he called down upon me all the blessings of Allah and his prophet Mahommed. And what a glorious day I spent. The different varieties of booze I sampled, and also food. When I arrived at the Anzac that night I had difficulty in finding my bed, and when eventually I did find it, it seemed to be running round and round and past me, and I had to wait to catch it coming back before I could get into it.

I had a nice fat head when I reported at the Citadel at nine o'clock next morning (having previously booked my bed for another night). I was told to give the chair another coat of paint, and report at nine o'clock the following morning.

Again I was free for the day, with money in my pocket and the joys of wonderful Cairo mine for the taking. Cairo! It seemed like paradise to me after the barren wilderness of the Judean Hills. Cairo, with its gorgeously-coloured throng in the bazaar, its mosques and minarets. The wonderful Nile with its Great Bridge, the wonderful drive in a native gharri through the miles of shaded highway to see that wonderful monument of the ancient Pharaohs of Egypt, the Great Pyramid and Sphinx.

Next morning at nine I reported again to the master painter, and by the application of another coat of paint I finished my chair and was told I had passed my test and was given twenty four hours leave.

Again I booked a bed at the Anzac and spent the rest of the day enjoying myself with the remains of my five hundred piastres. The next morning I reported to the R.T.O. and proceeded to El-Kantara where I spent the night, entraining next morning for Ludd. On arrival here I went to the rest camp at Latrun, where I stayed for ten days, owing to the movements of my battalion being uncertain.

I eventually re-joined my unit just outside Nablus, after an absence of nearly four weeks to paint a chair. Four weeks and a journey of several hundred miles to do a task that took at most about three hours. Truly, the ways of the Army Heads are strange and wonderful. But should I worry? I should say not, for to a soldier in Palestine a trip to Cairo is the equivalent – almost – of a trip to Blighty for a soldier in France.

Advance over the Jordan

At the end of April our division (the 60th) descended into the Jordan Valley, crossed the River Jordan by the newly-constructed bridge and bivouacked.

On the night of 30th April our battalion moved up and at dawn on the 1st May we came into contact with the Turkish outposts. After a sharp skirmish these fell back on their main body, and then a general action began with the object of driving Johnny Turk from his position in the foothills, our objective being Rifle Hill.

It soon became apparent that the Turks were there in strong numbers (it became known later that they were greatly reinforced by German troops). We rushed and captured their first line, and surprised and captured many men and officers in their bivouacs. But for a time it seemed we could get no further, so we consolidated our position and waited.

The heat was terrific, and lying down behind our scanty cover we were soon the object of attention of swarms of flies who tortured us almost beyond endurance, and as every move we made to ease our lot brought forth bursts of machine gun fire at us, we had perforce to lie still and endure the attentions of these pests.

Just at the back of me a dead Turk was stretched face to the sky. At least I suppose it was his face, but it was hard to say with certainty for it was black with flies, who were having a glorious time apparently. I noticed he had no boots on, but pieces of canvas wound round his feet and secured with string, and most of his equipment seemed held together with string. Evidently the Turkish troops were getting in a bad way since they started their retreat from Jerusalem.

I had a terrible thirst, but very little water in my bottle and no knowing when I would get any more, so I had to resist the temptation to have a swig at its brackish lukewarm contents. Oh for a good drink of ice-cold water, like it used to come from the tap in the back yard at home in Blighty. And oh! these cursed flies that try to get up your nose, into your eyes, and into your very mouth. And the lice sticking to the pools of sweat in the hollow of your chest.

My mate Budge, lying next to me, nudges my elbow. "How's it going, Jimmy? Pretty ghastly, eh? Here, take a swig at this. But don't move about too much, or Johnny will send us some of his crackers".

I glance towards him and pick up the flask he has laid beside me. I take a swig. Ah, brandy! It goes down grand. Puts new life in me. I return it to the ground beside him. "Thanks, Budge! That was grand. Where did you win that from?"

"Ah never you mind Jimmy, as long as I got it" he replied as he replaced it in his haversack. Budge was a masterpiece at getting possession of a flask of something or other. Sometimes whisky, sometimes brandy, rum or benedictine. Or, if nothing better was obtainable, vin blanc or vin rouge. I don't think he'd have turned up his nose at methylated spirits. He was almost as good as poor old Ted Castell at getting hold of a bottle of daddy's comfort.

Poor old Ted. I expect he's finished with the war for good, after that packet he copped at Messines Ridge, when I had to leave him lying after he'd got a second wound. Or perhaps he was napooed. That wound in the head looked pretty bad. I'd heard no news of him since, so....

My thoughts are interrupted by Corporal Bourne near me, shouting "Look out! I think they're comin'!" followed by bursts of machine gun fire and shrapnel shells bursting right over our heads. This looks like the overture to a counter-attack. We crouch down even closer to the earth, as the hornets of death whistle over our heads and the shrapnel splinters whine by with a vicious sound like a swarm of angry bees.

"Look out, here they come. Let 'em have it, boys! Rapid fire!" Rat-tat-tat, tat-tat-tat, tat-tat-tat, barked the Lewis guns, and our rifles kept up their non-stop chatter.

Johnny Turks dropping in scores, amidst yells of "Allah! Allah! Al Allah! Allah Akabar!" Only a few reach our line, and these are soon settled. The Turks are crawling back to their position, all except those who will never crawl again, and there are scores of these lying in front. Johnny has had enough.

Corporal Bourne is dead beside me, copped one clean through the head. I turn round to see if Budge is alright and then I feel as if someone has hit me on the leg with a mallet. I see blood streaming down my leg. I am wounded.

Budge shouts "You're hit, Jimmy! Crawl back to the aid post. Tat-ta! Good luck, Jimmy". I pull out my field dressing and hastily bandage the wound – just above my right knee – and crawl back to the aid post, which is under cover behind a rise in the ground.

Here, with many others, I am re-bandaged and ticketed and then we start off on our walk to the casualty clearing station at Jericho. It is a long tramp across the plain and after about an hour we arrived at a tributary of the Jordan. I knelt down and drank water like a horse, till I thought I should burst, and then I filled my bottle. Many of the others did the same. A little further up the stream we saw some Arabs washing clothes in the stream we had just drunk from.

Eventually we arrived at the clearing station, where we were given tea and bread and bully beef and put into an ambulance en route for the hospital in Jerusalem. Here we spent the night, and next morning proceeded to the railway station and were put in a train consisting of cattle trucks with straw on the floor, in which we journeyed to the general hospital at Gaza. Here I remained for five weeks, and then being pronounced fit I was sent with a number of others to the base depot at El-Kantara.

On arrival here I was given the job of servant to some officers who had just come over from Blighty. This was a nice cushy job. Not much to do, just to take them an early morning cup of tea at half past five, clean up their tents after they went on parade and do a bit of washing for them. For this job I got extra pay and a good tip when they left the base to go up the line.

After I had been at this for a fortnight, the whole of my battalion arrived at the base and I was ordered to join them. Here I learnt that on account of the German offensive in France, all available white troops were to leave Palestine and proceed to France.

About a week later our battalion embarked at Alexandria and sailed to Taranto in Italy, after which, at the end of a ten days' journey in cattle trucks through the land of macaroni and ice-cream, we arrived at Calais just as Jerry was making an air raid on the station.

We went into billets for a fortnight's rest, where we were inspected by the army corps commander, who called us a "battalion of scarecrows". I expect we looked so, with our torn clothing and the best part of the men covered in sores. Anyhow, we were patched up and sent in reserve up the line on the Kemmel sector.

Reflection No. 8

FRANCE AGAIN

Jerry's big offensive had failed and he was now in retreat. So far, our battalion had not been called on to do much on account of our poor condition after our Palestine service. Mostly we held reserve positions. While we were on reserve in the village of Saint-Sylvestre-Cappel I was troubled very much by attacks of sickness and diarrhoea and reported sick.

After several days of excused duty, the M.O. said to me "I think you're practically worn out and also suffering from enteritis, so I'm sending you to hospital. Get your kit packed up". A few hours later I was at the Canadian casualty clearing station, where I stayed for a couple of days and was then sent to hospital at Etaples.

After remaining here for a few days I was sent to another hospital, at Trouville on the coast. This was a special kind of hospital and not many cases were lucky enough to get to Blighty from here, as they reckoned to keep you until you were well enough to be sent back to the line again.

However, I managed to get into the good books of the sister in charge of my ward by doing little services for her. On one occasion one of the patients was short of his ration of fried fish for his tea, which had been ordered for him by the M.O., and made himself a nuisance, threatening to report it to the Medical Officer next morning.

The sister was in a bit of a stew about it, so as I was on the same diet as the man without his fish, I quietly called her over and gave her mine to give him, telling her I could manage quite well on the bread and butter alone. She was very thankful to get out of the bother and never forgot me for stepping into the breach.

Shortly after this she surprised me one morning just before the M.O.'s visit, by ordering me to get into bed. As I was not a bed patient, but had been dodging about the ward doing odd jobs, sometimes even helping to scrub the floors, I was not a little bewildered by the order. But I didn't argue, but got undressed and jumped into kip.

A few minutes later the M.O. came round on his daily visit and soon he and the sister stopped at my cot. "And how's this boy?" said the M.O.

"Well, Sir" said sister, "I think he's a thorough wreck. Properly worn out".

"How do you feel, son?" asked the M.O.

"Not very grand Sir" I said, playing up to the sister's lead. "No appetite, and I feel washed out and weak".

"What's his diet, Sister?"

"Just a little milk and rice, Sir".

"Been out in Palestine, haven't you?"

"Yes, Sir".

"How long have you been in the army?"

"Four years, Sir".

"Been wounded at all?"

"Four times, Sir".

"Well you seem to have had your share of it, sonny. Give me his board, Sister. There, that's that".

And he handed back the medical sheet to the sister, who hung it over the bed and passed on with the M.O. to the next cot. After the M.O. had gone, the sister came over to me and said "Well, James, you are marked by the M.O. as a stretcher case for the boat for England. You'll be leaving us tomorrow. Are you sorry?"

I tried to thank her, but she would listen to none of it. So I gave her as a souvenir the buckle of a Turkish infantryman's belt, which I had carried about for months. The next morning I was carried out to the hospital ship, arrived at Southampton in the evening and was despatched to the Auxiliary Military Hospital at Griffithstown, Monmouthshire.

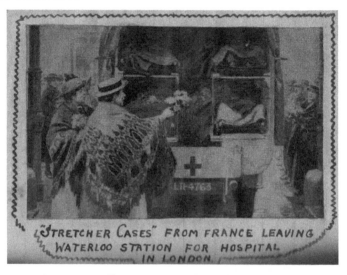

"STRETCHER CASES" FROM FRANCE LEAVING WATERLOO STATION FOR HOSPITAL IN LONDON.

A magazine illustration pasted into the manuscript

Reflection No. 9
THE END OF IT ALL

The hospital at Griffithstown (a small town in the mining district of Monmouthshire) to which I was sent was in pre-war days the local workhouse. There were about one hundred sick and wounded there, and the only places of entertainment were the local picture palace, a small bagatelle and billiard hall, and the YMCA hut.

If we wanted to go to a music hall we took a walk to Pontypool (about two miles distant), where we wounded and sick men were admitted free on the first house Friday to Pitts Theatre of Varieties.

Also, there were several pubs in that town. We were not supposed to be served in these places (the proprietors had orders to serve no Boys in Blue, meaning of course us wounded Tommies).

We got over that obstacle alright when we wanted a pint (which was pretty often) by turning the collar of our khaki overcoat up and putting on a pair of puttees to hide the bottoms of our blue hospital trousers, and completing the job by putting in our cap the badge of the local regiment, the South Wales Borderers.

A sergeant, who was a patient in the ward where I was, conceived the idea of forming a concert party. I put my name down and shortly, when we were about eight strong, we began rehearsing at the YMCA.

I paired up with a fellow named Brailey, of the Somerset Light Infantry, and we called ourselves the Brothers Desmond. We were rehearsing a sketch, Brailey and I, called "A Sister to Assist 'Er" which had been played in pre-war days by Fred Emney and Sydney Fairbrother. I played the part of the landlady and Brailey was Mrs May and her rich sister.

This coloured drawing by Walter James may depict
Brailey and himself performing "A Sister to Assist 'Er"

When we were all perfect in our various turns, we called ourselves the Blue Boys Concert Party. The sergeant had bills printed and displayed in the town something after this fashion. (The first show was given at a place known as Saint Hilda's Hall, Griffithstown).

The concert was a great success, and we sold about forty pounds worth of our tickets. The YMCA had a good sum towards their funds, after the hire of the hall was paid for, and each member of the concert party had received seven and sixpence each for refreshments.

Our manager (the sergeant) then started getting busy, and booked up concerts at various halls amongst which were the Town Hall, Abergavenny, White Star Cinema, Pontnewyyd, and the Empire Theatre, Abersychan.

After a time several members of the concert party were discharged from hospital, and so the Blue Boys came to an end.

I then started a party consisting of myself and two more, which I called the Desmond Trio. I had tickets printed and made dates at the various pubs around Pontypool. The tickets were sold (at 9d each) and we turned up on the date given and done our stuff. I would open the show with a couple of comic songs, "The End of my Old Cigar" and "What a Funny Little Place to have One". Then one of the other members of the trio would sing and play on the piano, after which I would do a double turn with the other member, introducing the old cross-talk comedians stuff.

After a time members of the audience would give songs, and just before chucking-out time the guvnor of the pub would settle up with us as regards the ticket money, give us a parting pint and we would make tracks for the hospital, climb over a fence (for the hospital gates closed at nine) and jump into bed as quick as we could. (The sister always turned a blind eye to our stunts).

At the end of January 1919 I was discharged from hospital and returned to civil life. Later, I received a pension and a discharge certificate stating I was discharged under Para/392 XVI (KR). "No longer fit for service, having suffered impairment since entry into the service".

THE END

APPENDIX: FURTHER INFORMATION ON SOME INDIVIDUALS MENTIONED IN THE TEXT

SERGEANT TATTERSALL ("TATERS")

Frank Alfred Tattersall enlisted in September 1914 with the service number 2759. He was killed at the Somme on 15th September 1916 aged 24. Walter saw him fall and instinctively wanted to stop, but he would have been under orders to continue walking across No Man's Land until reaching enemy lines. Frank has no known grave and is commemorated on the Thiepval Memorial.

Frank was born in Southsea, Hampshire in 1891, to Alfred Tattersall, a draper's assistant, and Emily Ellen (née King). By the time of the 1901 census the family are at 85 Halley Road, Forest Gate and Alfred is a commercial traveller. Ten years later Emily, now describing herself as a "deserted wife", has taken Frank and his younger sisters Maud and Muriel to live at 8 George Street in her home town of Romford. This would be Frank's home until his death.

SERGEANT F. A. TATTERSALL, age twenty-four, who was killed in action on 15th September, 1916, while serving with the London Regiment, entered the Company's service in the Audit Department on 27th December, 1905.

His obituary in the Great Eastern Railway Magazine

MR. F. A. TATTERSALL.

83

Before the war Frank was a clerk in the Great Eastern Railway Audit Department. He is commemorated on the GER War Memorial at Liverpool Street Station. His name also appears on Romford's War Memorial in Coronation Gardens, close to the Town Hall. Number 8 George Street was demolished to make way for a ring road in the late 1960s, but Frank's former home at Halley Road still stands.

SERGEANT HULLAND

Reginald Percy Hulland (service numbers 2173 & 320548) became platoon sergeant following the death of Frank Tattersall and was awarded the Military Medal for bravery. He was born in May 1892 in Hornsey, Middlesex, and before enlisting worked as a showroom assistant with the South Metropolitan Gas Company. He survived the war, married Sarah Compton in 1921 and lived to the grand age of 89.

RIFLEMAN POWELL ("THE POLE CAT")

The name Powell is sometimes pronounced Pole, so Pole Cat would be a suitable punning nickname for Walter's comrade, "a greedy cuss...always in possession of the finest collection of lice in the whole battalion".

We mentioned in the introduction that these Reflections were written many years after the events, which affected Walter's recall of certain details. The date of the Pole Cat's death seems to be an example. We're told that he was killed by a grenade in the aftermath of a German attack. Walter writes "Our division lost so heavily in this attack that we are ordered out of the line for a month to get up to strength again". He gives the date as 21st May 1916.

Evidence would suggest, however, that in fact it occurred on 30th April. The Cast Iron Sixth war diary for that date describes an attack that "more or less obliterated" part of the front line, leaving the battalion with 24 killed, 51 wounded and 17 missing. The Commonwealth War Graves Commission records the number of dead as 44. One of these is a George William Powell (service no. 4896), who lies buried at Cabaret-Rouge British Cemetery at Souchez. No-one named Powell belonging to the battalion was killed on 21st May.

Finally, Walter recalls this episode taking place not long after he came back from sick leave. According to his medal rolls information he returned to France at the beginning of April 1916, not in May as he had thought.

"TUG" WILSON and JIMMY HURST

Walter writes that as he awaits the signal to go over the top on 15th September 1916, "My thoughts turn to Jimmy Hurst and Tug Wilson, home on leave in Blighty. Ah! they were lucky. They had escaped this lot alright".

From information on the CWGC website, we have tentatively identified them as Albert Wilson (service no. 322236) and Alexander Edwin Richard Hirst (3367 and 32126). Unknown to him, they must have been recalled from leave to take part in the attack. Both were killed that morning. They have no known graves, and their names are commemorated on the Thiepval Memorial.

TED CASTELL

Ted is a colourful character, a "champion scrounger" who carries rum in his water bottle and confides to Walter that in civilian life he was a burglar! Ted received a bad head wound at Messines Ridge on 7th June 1917. Walter heard no more of him after that, and feared he had died.

We're unable to positively identify Ted, but the most likely candidate is Frederick Charles Cattle (service no. 322962) who died of wounds aged 31 in Newport General Hospital, Wales, on 23rd December 1917 and is buried at Islington Cemetery. He was a compositor by trade, which reminds us that the Cast Iron Sixth was founded as the Printers' Battalion, hence its nickname based on the use of "hot metal" type. He married Nellie Elizabeth Noone in 1912 and they lived at 39 Skinner Street, Clerkenwell with their daughter Winifred, born in 1915.

poor old ted ... I expect he's finished with the war for good .. after that packet he copped at messines Ridge. .... when I had to leave him lying after he'd got a second wound.... or perhaps he was 'napooed' ... that wound in the head looked pretty bad .. I'd heard no news of him since

The writer wondering what happened to his friend Ted

Index of names and places mentioned in the text

CPSIA information can be obtained
at www.ICGtesting.com
Printed in the USA
BVHW022003011121
620462BV00018B/421

9 781911 391098